©2023 Inspire

a publication of Business in Heels International Pty Ltd

All rights reserved.

No portion of this book may be reproduced, stored in a retrieval system, or transmitted in any form or by any means – electronic, mechanical, photocopy, recording or scanning, or other – except for brief quotations in critical reviews or articles without prior permission of the authors and Business in Heels International Pty Ltd.

All rights reserved with the authors ©Business in Heels International Pty Ltd co-authors:

Faye Bendrups
Michelle Stankiewicz
Jolene Morse
Sheetal Pillai
Clare Jobson
Toni Knight
Leonie Noble

For further information and any questions visit our
Website www.businessinheels.com
Email info@businessinheels.com

ISBN: 978-0-6451639-4-0 (paperback)

Typeset & design by Karinya Kreations, Design Studio
www.kkreations.design

Edited by Steve Sweeney

Compiled, produced, and published by
Business in Heels International Pty Ltd

Contents

Foreword by Lisa Sweeney — 7

Faye Bendrups — 11
   Disaster Response in Peru
   A journey with people and passion — 13

Michelle Stankiewicz — 23
   Embracing the unknown — 25

Jolene Morse — 35
   The power of transformation — 37

Sheetal Pillai — 45
   Triumph of the Soul:
   A journey of resilience and empowerment — 47

Clare Jobson — 57
   From Grief to Growth:
   Empathy my superpower ... and my curse — 59

Toni Knight — 69
   The ironic path beyond burnout — 71

Leonie Noble — 81
   From boat to boardroom — 83

Other books in the series — 93

Foreword by
Lisa Sweeney

Welcome to our latest compilation book, "Inspire: A Life of Purpose," where we embark on a remarkable journey through the stories of seven courageous women. In the following pages, we delve into their lives, their triumphs, their challenges, and the indomitable spirit that defines them. Through their experiences, we find inspiration that transcends the boundaries of gender, age, and circumstance.

Stories are the most powerful way to share ideas, and they have the unparalleled power to transform. As you immerse yourself in the narratives of these remarkable women, you'll come to understand the profound impact that stories can have on shaping our perceptions and expanding our horizons. Each story shared within these pages is a testament to the strength of the human spirit, demonstrating that resilience, determination, and a sense of purpose can overcome even the most daunting of obstacles. What sets the authors of this compilation apart is their remarkable bravery. It takes immense courage to be vulnerable, to open up about some of life's most challenging moments. Each author has fearlessly chosen to share their own journeys, complete with struggles and vulnerabilities, to offer a lifeline of hope and empathy to others. By baring their hearts and souls, they create a powerful connection that resonates deeply with readers, reminding us all that our shared human experiences unite us in our strength and resilience.

"Business in Heels" compilation books have proven time and again that they possess the remarkable ability to change lives. They offer a platform for voices that might have otherwise remained unheard, allowing others to resonate with shared experiences and discover that they are not alone on their journey. These books serve as beacons of hope and guidance, offering a roadmap for navigating life's challenges and opportunities. By normalizing diverse experiences, they empower individuals to embrace their uniqueness and find the courage to pursue their passions.

"I am proud to be an author of my own story that you can find in our first book 'Raw.' It was only a week after we released it that I was contacted by a reader who said it had changed her life. She had been very depressed and upon reading my story, very like her own, had found a different way to handle things." This anecdote illustrates the transformative potential of sharing our stories. It speaks to the ripple effect that vulnerability and authenticity can have, creating a network of support and inspiration that transcends the boundaries of time and space.

As you read through the pages of "Inspiration: A Life of Purpose," I invite you to not only witness the transformative power of these stories but to also recognize the potential for transformation within yourself. These narratives have been carefully curated to uplift, enlighten, and encourage, with the hope that they will ignite a spark within you—a spark that propels you towards embracing your own journey with renewed purpose and vigour.

May the stories shared here serve as a reminder that within every individual lies the capacity to create change, to overcome adversity, and to lead a life of purpose. So, open these pages with an open heart and an open mind, and allow the voices of these courageous women to touch your soul, inspire your thoughts, and guide you on your own path of purpose.

Enjoy!

Lisa Sweeney

| CEO, Business in Heels International Pty Ltd

Website www.businessinheels.com

"Suddenly, in the middle of the formalities, Lima was hit with a 5.4 earthquake. All the scenario training was immediately put to good use..."

Faye Bendrups

ABOUT THE AUTHOR

Faye **Bendrups**

I have had what is termed a portfolio career. I've been (and still am) a performance-maker, writer, composer, academic researcher, teacher, emergency volunteer. This has allowed me fantastic opportunities to live a life that is stimulating, full of discovery, has room for great collaborations, and allows me to put back in to society.

I began my working life in the performing arts and many of my original works have been commissioned by major Australian companies. I received the Medal of the Order of Australia (OAM) for services to the performing arts. I went back to study in my 40s, completed an MA then a PhD in Latin American Studies, and worked for universities in Australia and overseas.

My work has been recognised with various awards; including the Victorian Premier's Volunteer Leadership award, the National Emergency Medal

ABOUT THE AUTHOR

and been named as '100 Women of Influence' by the Australian Financial Review, but really the most important thing to me is that I can look at myself in the mirror and know I have done stuff that matters.

In the emergency services, I've been an operational first responder with the State Emergency Service for 17 years. I have mentored emerging leaders, increased diversity and inclusion, advocated for cultural change, and contributed to national emergency strategic planning and development, as President of the Victoria SES Volunteers Association and Vice Chair of the National SES Volunteers Association. My chapter is a story about my experience participating in disaster and emergency response exercises in Peru.

Facebook	facebook.com/faye.bendrups
LinkedIn	https://au.linkedin.com/in/dr-faye-bendrups-oam-7a92203b
Bus. website	tangomundo.org

by Faye Bendrups

Disaster Response in Peru
A Journey with People and Passion

"Come on Faye. You have to be up the front with the General."

Lima, Peru, 2014. I had been here before, during the time of the *sendero luminoso* guerillas' reign of terror with bombs in the city, tanks and armed forces on guard, and muted conversations on street corners. General Alfredo Murgueytio Espinoza had been seen as a hero for his part in routing the rebels and restoring the country to the rule of law and democracy. Now he was head of INDECI, the National Institute for Civil Defence, and I was in Lima on an official visit to participate in a series of disaster scenario exercises. And José Ambía, Chief of the Office of Co-operation and International Affairs, was directing me to stay up front with the boss.

The day started out with the regular Lima warmth and humidity but was getting hotter. I had just arrived at the last minute, due to plane delays and breakdowns out of both Sydney and Auckland, so my well-prepared 2 days in advance time to acclimatise had evaporated and I had not slept for 72 hours. And here I was, decked out in a formal SES dress uniform

by Faye Bendrups

of long-sleeved thick shirt and tie, heavy woollen pants and blazer while preparing to run alongside the General at the front of a whole school, the Minister for Education and his staff, other officials, media, and key members of INDECI while conducting a disaster scenario of an incoming tsunami which could result in 50,000 casualties and with only 15-20 minutes to escape to higher ground.

The General set the pace at the front to a medium jog. I ran alongside and was impressed, not only at his fitness, but at his involvement at the grassroots. Here was the most senior emergency leader in the nation choosing to start the day of community disaster exercises not by sitting in his air-conditioned office overseeing the procedures remotely, but by participating alongside a cohort of school students and being the example to inspire them. (Note to self: no time for exhaustion and heat, step up and keep up. There was no place to hide as the international press from across the Americas was covering the General's day and TV cameras were everywhere.)

Around 17 minutes later, the General's steady jog, without missing a beat, had led us across busy highways (traffic just gave way), through local suburbs (residents joined us), and up hills to the safe zone. The primary school children bringing up the rear had linked together by holding onto a long rope with their teachers. There was no panic, acting up or misdirected energy. It was routine and taken seriously. Across the nation, around 8 million students had participated in similar scenarios.

"Faye, you must give some commentary to everyone about their performance!" José advised, handing me the megaphone. A couple of challenges here. One, my Spanish was okay for informal conversations but not up to technical advice on emergency response while being filmed for national TV only hours after

by Faye Bendrups

arriving in Peru. Two, what should I say? That the pace was great? That most people made it, but some would have died?

The first challenge was solved by my partner Guillermo who was accompanying me on this trip as my official interpreter. He softly recommended some key sentences to use. The second was more difficult. In Australia, many emergency services leaders are reluctant to speak plainly about risk, injury, and death, possibly fearing it will panic the population or that they will not understand how to react. This in part is true. We do not have a strong and effective participatory culture around disasters and emergencies, even though we are regularly exposed to catastrophic events. Here in Peru, it was different...

The whole of community is involved in disaster preparedness. They practise throughout their lives. It is legislated that all schools conduct disaster scenario exercises 4 times a year, one of them at night, and that all communities conduct an additional 4 scenario exercises annually. There are also cross-border exercises with Chile and Bolivia. These are not passive desktop tick-and-flick procedures. They are full-blown, realistic drills with finely tuned timings and actions devised by INDECI. In simple terms, the procedure is like this: a whole of nation exercise will be scheduled for a particular date and time, the people will be informed of the scenario, and at the appointed time, millions of people stop their regular activities and participate. As it is normalised in this way, people are mentally prepared and have rehearsed their response many times. This means that in a major disaster, the general population can look after themselves for the initial response leaving the emergency services to deal with the most serious rescues.

by Faye Bendrups

How different to Australia! Here, emergency agencies are often under-resourced for major disasters and, while they expect the community to share the responsibility, there is no systematic approach to educating them and giving them the knowledge and confidence to manage themselves.

This was why I was in Peru.

I wanted our agencies to develop a more systematic, co-ordinated, and universal approach that was simple, achievable, and not rooted in red tape. I had been awarded a scholarship by the Emergency Services Foundation for this purpose and my heart was in it.

Back in Lima. That day, and the following 7 weeks, progressed rapidly. INDECI assigned us a personal driver, scheduled a series of meetings with heads of agencies, and involved me in all their strategic planning meetings and briefings. Overnight, I had become the international expert observer. I had gone from passenger to driver's seat in an instant! I was treated with incredible respect for my interest in their systems and for having made the trip from the other side of the world. I was the first emergency responder ever from Australasia to do so. And I certainly had to switch my thinking from being a local volunteer in Australia. In Peru, I was giving input from a national strategic perspective, consulting with diplomats, military personnel, scientists, and response leaders.

The schedule of activities was wide-ranging:
- an evacuation drill of thousands of people downtown in the world heritage-listed heart of Lima
- participating in the Working Technical Committee on Forest Fires
- observations at the National Emergency Operations Centre
- discussions with the Director and the Chief Scientist and Seismologist at the Peru Institute of Geophysics

by Faye Bendrups

- meetings with the Director of the Red Cross and the Fire Services Head of USAR (Urban Search and Rescue)
- attending the Technical Committee of the National Humanitarian Network (a multi-agency forum with visiting United Nations personnel)
- consulting with the Directorate of Development and Human Capacitation
- field trips to the Lucre district to assess flood recovery. (A visit to the Ubinas volcano – one of Peru's 3 most dangerous – was off limits as it had become active!)
- being invited to give a guest presentation on disaster and bushfire management in Australia which was attended by every functional director of INDECI.

Word had spread quickly: "There's an Australian woman here wanting to know everything." Soon I was referred to the National Service for Protected Parks and the Environment, learning about intercultural education in the Amazon Region and cultural conservation in Macchu Picchu. At short notice, they contacted their remote area park rangers in the Macchu Picchu Historic Sanctuary and organised for us all to meet at the ranger station at Piscacucho, often referred to as Km82, the start of the Inca Trail. It is almost 3,000m above sea level, in the Cusco region. We just needed to organise a quick flight to Cusco. Once there, National Parks supplied a driver and 4WD for the 2-hour journey to Piscacucho, taking the opportunity to load up the vehicle with food and other supplies we could deliver. For the rangers, it was far more difficult. One even trekked 6 hours on foot from his remote post to the nearest village, then travelled by bus the following day to reach Piscacucho.

These park rangers commit to a 12-month stint off the beaten track, to any of Peru's national parks, not

by Faye Bendrups

necessarily near their homes. They are rostered on for 22 days straight, then have a 4-day break during which they may return to their home, or if that is too far, their family may come to them. They are responsible for remote area firefighting (trained by a US aid program) and first aid (trained by doctors from Spain) and are often the only medical assistance for local villages. Some stations are accessible by 4WD, others only on foot from the nearest village which may be a 4-hour trek each way. Resources may be transported by donkeys or horses along inhospitable mountain trails. The rangers are critical to the national economy as tourism is Peru's third largest industry and second largest employer. The iconic Macchu Picchu, a UNESCO World Heritage site and voted one of the New Seven Wonders of the World, attracts up to 4,500 visitors daily.

In the relative comfort of the ranger station, we met and shared experiences and operational response approaches. Emergency activities in this territory are a formidable challenge; inaccessible and remote terrain, high altitude, snow and sub-zero temperatures, landslides, precipitous rivers, scrub fires and underground fires burning for months at a time. Not to mention rescuing and evacuating injured tourists, carrying all equipment for hours through the rugged mountain wilderness. We trekked off to sites of recent landslide and fire events, met local Quechua-speaking villagers and visited Inca ruins not accessible to the public. (Let me take a pause here and acknowledge the support of my partner Guillermo. While I have spent a good deal of time trekking in remote areas and doing other adventurous activities, he is a city person, pursuing the life of the mind! What had I dragged him into??)

Eventually, it was back to the city and more meetings. Of particular interest to me was the answer to this question... Why are their community engagement

by Faye Bendrups

programs so effective? I think the answer stems from everyone being engaged from an early age. Children and young people are actively included in planning and decision-making at every stage. This happens through the INDECI project Children and Adolescents Prepared in Responsive Disaster Risk Management, which is supported by UNICEF, Save the Children, the Education Department, Parliament, and other organisations. The objective is to develop and strengthen the leadership capacities and skills of young people, to respect their right to participate and bring their voice into agency planning.

Suddenly, in the middle of the formalities, Lima was hit with a 5.4 earthquake. All the scenario training was immediately put to good use. We grabbed vital possessions, moved to the designated strongest part of the building, moved outside when the tremors ceased to a secure open area and waited for the all clear.

What did I learn from this intensive action research?

First, like the remote area park rangers, if you are the only person on the spot, it is up to you. Never mind that I was not the equivalent of something like a Federal Director of Emergency Management in Australia; I was the only Australian there, so I had to be the expert. Never mind that I was a local volunteer, not a paid staffer in charge of national operations; I was the only one there, so had to be able to answer questions.

Second, observing General Murgueytio, I knew that a style of leadership that connected with the grassroots, that led a fluid bottom-up/top-down approach, that exited the comfort of the office and participated on the same level as the people he served, was something I would always emulate.

Third, when faced with challenges that required a quick response, whether it be to hop on a plane, trek in the mountains, give an impromptu speech, engage

by Faye Bendrups

with officials at the highest level of government, military, and diplomacy, or take action in an earthquake, then I would not hesitate to grasp that opportunity firmly with both hands. Why say no when you can always say yes?

I was humbled by the incredible support given to me by the Emergency Services Foundation, Guillermo, the Peruvian Ambassador to Australia, the Australian Ambassador to Peru, every department of INDECI in both Lima and Cusco and government ministries, to name a few. If it had been the other way round, would Australia have seen the value in giving a visiting first responder such attention? Would we have welcomed them to high-level strategic planning meetings? Supplied a private driver? Organised remote area meetings at short notice? Or persuaded 6 leading park rangers to leave their posts (at least one of whom had to walk for days to be there) to discuss operational techniques with an unknown female volunteer from a foreign country? I don't think I could have been better treated if I were the Prime Minister!

Back in Australia, I was able to carry through on implementing person-centred approaches to emergency management in my local area. I have been deployed to numerous local and interstate major disasters, including the 2019-2020 Black Summer bushfires. I have had broad engagement with my local community, particularly since the disastrous 2022 Maribyrnong River floods. There is still so much to do.

But something has kept bubbling away in the back of my mind: you see, I had a 7-week secondment to INDECI in Peru and it was a unique and deeply affecting experience. Their practises and procedures are impressive, with an emphasis on the culture of prevention, multicultural aspects of emergencies, and citizens' rights. Their level of active engagement is

by Faye Bendrups

astonishing and enshrined in their National Policy of Disaster Risk Management: "The best, most opportune and targeted help is that which comes from the community and from individuals themselves, especially in prevention, in self-awareness of exposure to risk, and in being prepared in order to minimise the consequences of a disaster."

What was simmering away in the back of my mind?

Why can't we do that here? Do we have a level of complacency? A dependence or passivity that inhibits individuals to respond effectively? Or is it a policy constraint?

Then I realised there was a fourth thing I had learnt in Peru: that all the people and activities I met with, observed, or participated in, were driven by dedication, commitment and the 'P' word, Passion. A word and concept that many people feel a little uncomfortable (even embarrassed) about using here in our wonderful, comfortable, wealthy, developed nation. Yet surely, it is the key to truly living to our full potential, understanding ourselves and creating our purpose in the world. My life and career, like everyone's, have been full of adventures and achievements as well as the failures and knockbacks. But working with INDECI confirmed for me that, whether in relation to disaster management or anything else, the determination to excel, contribute, share, set an example, influence and listen are the things that will sustain me and inspire me to be a more effective leader. And that complacency and indifference are the enemy.

And that we have a choice. So, it is up to us to choose wisely, fearlessly.

"Growing up, I did not fully appreciate my parent's resilience at overcoming hurdles. I overlooked the positivity, courage and energy required to survive, continually relocate, and reinvent themselves – boilermaker, machinist, welder, restaurant owner, canned goods manufacturer, boarding house owner/operator, baker, singer & restaurant supplier..."

Michelle Stankiewicz

ABOUT THE AUTHOR

Michelle
Stankiewicz

Michelle is a Career Management Professional and Executive Coach who works with individuals across a variety of sectors. These include not-for-profit, financial services, retail, technology, consumer products, and professional services. In a thought-provoking and creative process, she inspires clients to maximise their personal and professional potential.

Her strengths as a coach stem from her successful corporate career managing complex relationships and large-scale organisational change. Her strong background in people development, and her drive to help individuals achieve what matters most to them, led Michelle to refocus her own career on her passion for coaching as an independent Executive and Career Coach and as a consultant for leading Career Management consultancies.

Michelle's solution and strength-based approach supports individuals to gain clarity, build pathways

About the Author

to navigate change, and identify chosen career paths. She then coaches her clients to achieve their chosen goal: to secure a fulfilling role aligned with their chosen direction, to start their own business, or to move away from full time work.

Outside of her professional life, Michelle is passionate about bringing positive, lasting change to communities and works as a volunteer job advisor for the Newtown Asylum Seekers Centre and as a volunteer youth mentor with the Raise Foundation.

Michelle holds formal qualifications in Executive Coaching, Leadership, HR, Project Management, Education, ICT, Mental Health First Aid and Training and Assessment. Her advanced interpersonal skills are built on credibility, trust, and openness which she utilises to facilitate highly effective coaching outcomes under often challenging circumstances.

Specialties: Career Coaching, Executive Coaching, Resume, LinkedIn, Networking, Interviews, Job Search Strategy, Redeployment, Outplacement, Career Transition, Career Management.

Email	michellestankiewicz@gmail.com
LinkedIn	linkedin.com/in/michellestankiewicz
Qualifications	B.Ed., Organisational Executive Coaching, Human Resources, Project Management Diploma, NLP Practitioner, Positive Psychiatry, Science of Wellbeing, Mental Health First Aid, Cert IV Training and Assessment, Building your Career in Tomorrows Workplace, Leadership: Identity, Influence and Power (LEAD)

by Michelle Stankiewicz

Embracing the unknown

As a Polish man and Ukrainian woman with no English and no money, my parents embraced the unknown as they disembarked at Sydney's Circular Quay after fleeing war-torn Europe. In 1952 Australia, they were subjected to much racism and continually told to go back to where they came from. This was nothing compared to what they had already endured as, by this stage, they had experienced persecution, tragedy, starvation, and homelessness.

Having just finished high school in Ukraine, my mother's plans to study medicine were shattered when WW2 broke out and she was abducted from her small village by German soldiers. Tightly packed onto a goods train with many others, she was transported to rural Germany to work as forced labour. It was here that she met my father who had also been taken from his village in Poland under similar circumstances. He was later unjustly targeted and arrested by the Gestapo, imprisoned in a Nazi slave labour camp, and forced to dig a 100km railway tunnel on starvation rations. This difficult work, low

by Michelle Stankiewicz

rations and terrible conditions underground led to a high death rate. It brought tears to my eyes hearing that my father's weight rapidly dropped from 75kg to 41 kgs in 56 days. And what a frightening impact it must have had on him to witness the horror of daily firing squads for those trying to escape. It frustrated me that we never found out more as he refused to talk to us about these terrifying times, dismissing them as "*old history.*" At the same time, I understand how harrowing those memories must be. I can only imagine how their hearts must have been racing when the war ended, and they narrowly escaped being sent to Siberia by hiding in a haystack. And just when they would have been yearning to reconnect with friends and family, the distress and utter disappointment they must have endured would have been agonising when their families lovingly, yet reluctantly, encouraged them not to return to their home countries due to the grim political situation.

Their first child, my brother Harry, was born in a post-war displaced person's camp in Hannover, Germany. It still haunts me that Harry tragically died of food poisoning in the camp at only 6 months of age. It wasn't until my own children were born that the grief hit me. How devastating it must have been to bury your child and continue to embrace the unknown. Working their way across Europe, they saved up for the ship's fare that would take them to the other side of the world, to start their new life in Australia, far away from their homes and families.

Their first home in Australia was half a garage before moving into a room above a cafe which they ran. Their future was finally looking brighter, when, without warning, a fire broke out while they slept. It is chilling to picture how they only narrowly escaped with their lives by jumping out their first-floor window, losing everything and facing the daunting task of starting over... again.

by Michelle Stankiewicz

Growing up, I did not fully appreciate my parent's resilience at overcoming hurdles. I overlooked the positivity, courage and energy required to survive, continually relocate, and reinvent themselves – boilermaker, machinist, welder, restaurant owner, canned goods manufacturer, boarding house owner/operator, baker, singer & restaurant supplier. Success and stability finally came from building their successful catering business specialising in continental food for home and office functions using recipes from their homelands. Their food was novel and highly sought after in 1960's Sydney. They were in high demand, worked seven days a week and holidays were rare. As school holidays approached, my brother and I despaired each time we heard their familiar mantra: *"You can never turn away a booking as you never know when your next one will be."*

The story I told myself: Never have your own business. You'll never have a day off and you bear all the risk.

Growing up in this environment, I'd scavenge items from our local tip, dust them off and sell them in my primary school playground. During high school, I worked at the local supermarket and spent most weekends working in our family catering business, not realising the lessons I was learning on what it took to run a (mostly harmonious) highly successful business partnership.

My mother ruled the industrial kitchen they had built behind our house. She was the head chef, project manager and a calm presence amongst a thriving, chaotic yet somehow orderly business. My father was sous-chef. He knew his place and diligently followed my mother's food preparation instructions. He then transported food and equipment all over Sydney and managed a team of waiters and waitresses, many of whom had just landed in Australia and were hungry

by Michelle Stankiewicz

for work. I was in charge of making savouries and waitressing at some of the most exclusive homes in Sydney. As an introverted teenager, waitressing amongst strangers in unfamiliar environments was uncomfortable. My father worked by my side and watched out for me. I put myself through university with door-to-door sales, bar work and maths tutoring while continuing to work in the family business.

When I graduated with my teaching degree, I was the first university graduate in my family. My parent's pride must have turned to dismay when I told them that teaching was not my path. It was a troubling time for me, one of deep confusion and self-doubt. I was grateful that my parents kept their feelings to themselves and gave me the space I needed.

The story I told myself: Give space to others to allow them time to reflect and determine their own path.

It was 1982 and I had no idea what to do. How do I make the most of the opportunity my parents had made possible and never had themselves?

My Polish uncle was staying with us at the time. He was an astute businessman and the catalyst behind my parents choosing to migrate to Australia. His advice was that computers were taking off and I should pursue this path. I was instantly motivated by curiosity and the excitement of exploring an emerging industry. Why not?

It was not an easy start for a female with no IT qualifications. 40 years ago, it was an even more heavily male-dominated industry than it is today. I still recall the weight of the stress I felt being one of sixty (almost all-male) applicants, sitting psychometric and logical reasoning tests for a rare trainee computer operator job. Even when selected as one of the final three candidates, as the only female, I expected I had no chance. So, imagine my euphoria

by Michelle Stankiewicz

when chosen as the successful candidate. It was mind blowing! Even more so, since I was the first female the company had ever hired in their IT department.

At the time, I was unaware the head of the IT department had three daughters. It was not until many years later, that I reflected and realised why he had hired me. I tried to track him down to thank him, but he had sadly already passed away. I was devastated to have missed the opportunity to show my gratitude. I did, however, experience great joy in tracking down his daughters to share my story and thank them. Unsurprisingly, they were all successful in their own fields. I was deeply touched by their gratitude. It was wonderful to share the pivotal role their late father had played in my career and as an early advocate for gender diversity.

> The story I told myself: Now I need to learn how to "be" as the only female in this workplace.

Being the first female, the company had ever hired in their IT department generated further self-inflicted pressure. I had entered a very "blokey" environment and was on a steep learning curve. Filled with anxiety, I often needed to dig deep to ignore their pranks. After all, they were testing the waters and determining boundaries too. I had to help them recalibrate and be open to other perspectives and ways of working. Most importantly, I needed to gain respect through listening, learning, asking questions, consistently delivering, owning up to mistakes and contributing new ideas.

> The story I told myself: Don't stuff this up, this is an opportunity to pave the way for other females.

It was gratifying that the next three IT hires were all female. There was an instant shift in workplace culture, communication style and diversity of thinking. I was rapidly promoted to Computer

by Michelle Stankiewicz

Operations Supervisor and then moved into programming. When I resigned 3 years later to continue challenging myself and to broaden my skills, it was not just my IT skills which had grown. I felt accomplished, had conquered multiple fears, stretched myself and smoothed the path for others.

My curiosity and sense of adventure kicked in. I longed to learn more about the countries my parents once called home. With my then boyfriend (now husband) in tow, I spent a year in London working as a contract programmer followed by another year of discovery travelling the world. It fed my soul!

The story I told myself: Keep feeding your soul with travel, keep learning about who you are and stand on the shoulders of your parents' misfortune, strengths & power.

My inspirational parents had retired by the time I returned to Australia two years later. I spent the next 22 years at Qantas, growing my IT career in an organisation with a great cultural fit that supported my passion for travel. I enjoyed building IT systems for our iconic national brand, making the most of the employee travel benefits & being surrounded by smart, equally passionate colleagues. Gender diversity was no longer an issue. My next hurdle was surviving multiple redundancies in the volatile travel industry. Leaning into my parent's resilience, flexibility, and versatility, I continually reinvented myself and avoided multiple redundancies. I pivoted from writing code to supporting IT systems to leading teams of developers and becoming an IT Project Manager. I spent my final 5 years at Qantas managing the relationship between Qantas and the vendors to which most of IT had been outsourced. My two beautiful sons were then healthy teenagers and raising them had equipped me with the skills I needed for this job where the objective was to make everyone play nicely together.

by Michelle Stankiewicz

> The story I told myself: Transferable skills can be found in the most surprising places.

Tragedy struck when my amazingly strong, inclusive, and supportive parents both passed away as I turned 50. My elder care responsibilities had stopped but my world had become unstuck. As I worked through my grief, I started contemplating my own legacy and where I could find a different meaning and purpose.

> The story I now told myself: I don't want to die with any regrets.

My head was spinning with questions…

What did people come to me for? What did I enjoy at work? What did I no longer enjoy at work? When did IT drop from number 1 to 25 on the list of things I enjoyed? What would challenge me now?

Part of the latest redundancy package Qantas was offering included some coaching sessions with a career transition coach. It seemed the stars had aligned so I jumped into the great unknown.

I went into my first coaching session with an open mind, full of hope but with no ideas about my direction. Within the first 15 minutes, I had that "light bulb" moment. The rush of excitement was like a jolt of electricity. I stopped my coach mid-sentence to excitedly declare: "*Stop! I know what I want to do next. I want your job!*"

> The story I told myself: I want to see the magic that can happen helping others achieve their light bulb moment.

My husband describes this time as watching a freight train of sheer determination and drive. To me, it was a blur of highly focused activity and one of the most exciting times of my life. I was in complete control, and it was invigorating. Being truly in flow, I sought out and built connections with many beautiful and

by Michelle Stankiewicz

generous career coaches. I built my marketing plan and gained clarity on my direction. Having researched and identified the top 10 outplacement companies I wanted to work for, I mustered up the courage to introduce myself to them all and share my elevator pitch. My husband had lovingly stepped up to keep the household running which gave me the space I needed. I grew my confidence and expertise through training courses and lots of pro bono work helping my ex-colleagues get jobs by writing their resumes, advising on job search strategies, and preparing them for interviews. Two days after leaving Qantas, I secured my first paid career consulting work. I had also started my own career coaching business and was being referred private clients by word-of-mouth through my network.

My comfort zone and personal safety was temporarily tested by a short contract getting 40 long-term unemployed into jobs leading up to Christmas to prevent a job centre in a disadvantaged area of Sydney being shut down. I did it. However, having my life threatened, feeling constantly on edge and completely unprepared, I quickly realised this was not for me.

> **The story I told myself: It's OK to move back into your comfort zone, but don't stop testing your boundaries.**

Having kept up networking with my top 10 companies, 9 months after leaving Qantas, I secured my first permanent career consulting job at the number one company on my list. I was elated and would spend the next seven years there establishing an industry-first career transition centre embedded within a leading financial institution. Everything was going to plan...

Which, of course meant...

It was time to move out of my comfort zone again.

by Michelle Stankiewicz

My parents' experiences had taught me the importance of not needing all the answers to start with, and how to remain open-minded in the face of uncertainty and risk. So, my next challenge was to see if I could work entirely for myself. I approached a leading global career transition company where I now consult as a career coach alongside my private practice. I love it! It is exhilarating reflecting on how far I have come and how the story I tell myself has changed. I feel an incredible sense of gratitude, accomplishment, and pride at having been able to accept the fear and push through it as my parents had done.

The new story I told myself: Having your own business is OK if you love what you do, have clear work/life boundaries, and keep it flexible.

In 2020, my "no regrets" policy resurfaced meaning it was time to move out of my comfort zone again and make the most of my work flexibility. How could I honour my parent's legacy while also connecting with and giving back to my local community?

As a child of refugee parents, we often had new immigrants staying with us as my parents helped them find housing and employment. This helped me decide to leverage my new skills and volunteer as a job advisor at the Asylum Seekers Centre. It was uncomfortable at first to be working with people from a rich variety of cultures who had suffered real trauma. Yet with each humbling interaction, I became comfortable with the uncomfortable. It has given me a whole new level of respect and admiration for my parents as, 70 years ago, this was them. Somehow, they had still found the time and energy to love and raise me.

I come from a nurturing home and strong support network. Not all children are so lucky. Mental health for many young people is in crisis. Research shows that mentoring results in lower levels of depression

by Michelle Stankiewicz

and a higher sense of wellbeing. Knowing where to go for support also increases employment outcomes and future paths. This led me to volunteer as a youth mentor with Raise Foundation where I provide 1:1 mentoring at my local high school.

We all have different drivers. For me, it's my fear of missing out or having regrets. When you have a moment between your hustle and bustle, consider your drivers. It's a healthy exercise. Work is roughly a third of our lives and it's wonderfully liberating and motivating when we work at something which satisfies our core needs and values. Yet fear of change often prevents us from achieving this.

These days, my clients are the courageous ones who have reached their tipping point and are not content to live that way any longer. Turning the page is the best feeling, because there is so much more to your story than the page you are stuck on. The courage to accept change and embrace its opportunities brings great rewards.

It reminds me of a famous saying.

"Magic happens when we stop being afraid of what could go wrong, and start being excited about what could go right."

ABOUT THE AUTHOR

Jolene **Morse**

Born into a loving family as the youngest of four girls Jolene was taught early on that gender was not important to pursuing your dreams, instead with a natural sense of curiosity and a love of learning Jolene learnt the value of hard work and tenacity to chase your dreams.

Now, Jolene is a mother, a risk professional, a board member, an educator, a writer, a children's author, and a public speaker. Through a process of constant change, she has discovered her purpose and whilst she is still on her journey, she has learnt some critical lessons along the way, including that progress is never a linear process.

Jolene is passionate about all of the endeavours she undertakes and has an underlying drive to make a positive contribution to the world. Things that are worth achieving take time, perseverance and as Jolene has learnt through her journey to date – self-compassion. Life moves at a rapid pace and sometimes

ABOUT THE AUTHOR

it is easy to forget that sometimes, something as simple as brushing your teeth can be an achievement for that day. We should celebrate the small successes just as much as the large ones.

In her spare time Jolene loves being close to nature with her family – hiking, bike riding or sitting by an open fire.

Website | jolenemorsebooks.com.au

LinkedIn | linkedin.com/in/dr-jolene-morse-4302b6198

by Jolene Morse

The power of transformation

I was sitting on a beach in a stunning location. The sun was warm on my back, the ocean stretched out in front of me, and my family were playing in the sand as the waves rolled in. I had a good job, I was living a comfortable life, and there was no obvious reason for me not to feel completely content.

But as I sat there, watching the grains of sand pass through my fingers and seeing some of them stir in the breeze, I could not help but feel like one of them. A feeling washed over me like one of those rolling waves... although all the fundamentals were right, something was not where it needed to be and I was a little unstable. Something was starting to shift. What I didn't know was the journey this feeling would take me on and how the path I was about to walk would fundamentally change my view of the world.

To provide some context for how I got to this point and the journey until now, we need to look backwards to look forwards...

by Jolene Morse

After finishing my undergraduate degree, I commenced working fulltime in the finance industry. I was still not 100% sure which direction I would take and what I would specialise in. As I worked through various roles with a natural sense of curiosity, I wanted to learn and understand more about the industry and commenced postgraduate study to complement my working activities.

As I completed these initial studies, I realised I enjoyed the challenge of working and studying and being able to adapt, refine and challenge my thinking through this process. Accordingly, my sense was to undertake more study in the future. Yet for now, I wanted to focus on advancing my career.

With all this swirling around my mind, my boyfriend (now husband) and I were driving past the local university one day and we noticed an open day in progress. We decided to go in and explore Master's degree options. There was an older gentleman behind the postgraduate table observing us both standing there. He turned to my boyfriend and said, "How can I help you?" My boyfriend kindly informed him that he was not the one seeking information regarding studies. The gentleman then looked at me and said, "The undergraduate information is over there, love." I found the way he spoke to and treated me in comparison to my boyfriend both offensive and condescending. I collected all the forms for the Master's degree and decided there and then to apply to prove all this man's assumptions about me wrong. This turned out to be a pivotal moment for me.

Whilst my timing for initially applying to undertake the Master's degree had questionable motivating factors, the learning experience was very valuable and allowed me to apply the theoretical foundations in my "day job" and step into more senior, challenging roles. Working fulltime and studying was a challenging,

by Jolene Morse

but it was also very rewarding. It was at this time I realised how I liked to not only learn but to apply this and challenge assumptions and thinking whilst doing so.

I was standing in our kitchen with my husband when I received notification that I had successfully completed my Master's degree. I felt an enormous amount of pride and satisfaction. However, at that time I was also certain I did not want to study again until retirement many years in the future.

But you know how it works. Sometimes things do not go to plan……

I was discussing one of my friends commencing a doctorate with my husband one day and it sparked my curiosity. I wondered what the acceptance process would be. So, I started researching options, ended up applying and was accepted!! This was both exciting and terrifying. I did not know if I could manage a doctoral program with full-time work. But, I thought, there was only one way to find out. I accepted the place in the program and the next phase of my journey commenced.

The next few years of my life were a blur of working and researching and writing and…

Whilst I was already extremely busy, I was also ready to start a family. So, working under an assumption (false) that babies slept, I thought it would be manageable to start a family. When we were blessed and welcomed Sean into our lives, I soon learned some babies don't sleep, but are awfully sweet. Sean was a perfect addition to our family and added to the chaos of working and studying. Somehow, I continued with my journey and, prior to completing my doctorate, changed organisations and we also welcomed Kade into our family, who was equally sweet.

by Jolene Morse

It was a hectic few years. When I finally submitted my doctorate, I was relieved. And once again I said, "I would never study again." I was just going to do my day job from that point forward. However, from the time of submission to receiving notification that my research had been accepted, then walking across the stage at the graduation ceremony, I started to feel I was still not where I needed to be as a professional. Yes, there was still more to do.

It was at this point I found myself on the beach that day contemplating why I was not feeling more content. This really was the start of a transformational journey for me in many ways. In a very short time span after sitting on the beach that fateful day, I flipped my life on its head through factors both within and outside of my control.

I was contacted to present my research at two conferences, which was a terrifying thought for me! In parallel, I started applying for board positions, looking at academic roles and contemplating a career pivot and all of this was bubbling away as the COVID pandemic took hold.

They say people fear public speaking more than death itself and I firmly fell into this category. On the flip side, it was also something I really wanted to do. I accepted the opportunities to speak with a mixture of fear and excitement, with fear being by far the dominant emotion. Whilst preparing my slides and notes, I had so many doubts running through my head.

What if I sound stupid?

What if they think I am not adding any value?

What if I trip over going up the steps to speak?

by Jolene Morse

All were possibilities! But I specialise in risk management, I know there is a clear distinction between fear-based decision making and risk-based decision making. I stopped the negative fear-based thinking and started thinking, "What is the worst thing that can happen?" The answer was clear, if all my fears come to fruition, I simply won't be asked back to speak. When I thought about it in this context, failing was not going to be life changing but succeeding and trying could be. I got up on that stage and tried my best and none of my fears were realised. I was very fortunate to have this opportunity when I did because soon after the pandemic hit hard.

Also at this time, wheels I'd set in motion months ago began to gain traction. I was appointed to two boards, took a contract role to write and teach some academic content for a Master's program and changed my day job. This all occurred within six months of the start of the pandemic.

This may seem like a lot. Let me tell you... it was. I was totally uncomfortable with the pace of change and what I was doing. On the other side of this equation, these were all things I had always wanted to do. I had simply never had the courage to take that leap. And that is why I was feeling discontent on the beach that day. My fears. You see, up to that point, I had let fear control a part of my trajectory. I know, this is completely normal. We all do it. Our minds go to that space of worst-case scenarios first rather than thinking about the upside. This is evident in the work I do every day. So, I resolved to make a change in managing my thinking and this is where I had some additional pivotal moments.

The role I had stepped into as part of this transformational journey was amazing and I felt like it was where I needed to be. Approximately twelve months into this role, I was very fortunate to

by Jolene Morse

be selected to attend the Chief Executive Women's leadership program. Amongst other things, this involved undertaking a strengths assessment. This assessment showed my key strengths as a learner (somebody who has a desire to learn and continuously improve) and achiever (a desire to work hard with a great deal of stamina and taking immense satisfaction in being busy and productive).

Initially, I felt confused by these results because these things were supposed to be my strengths, yet they were all things I had been criticised for in the past. "I shouldn't work so hard." "I shouldn't be so busy." "I shouldn't be so…" But on the final day of what I can only describe as a life-changing course, I was speaking with one of the facilitators about my results. I was expressing my confusion about the results because these were attributes I had long suffered criticism for. She said some words to me that would change the way I viewed the world. "These are your strengths. This is who you are. Without these things, you would not be you and if people do not support you or understand that then they do not see you."

Wow.

Through tears and reflection, I realised how profound this was for me because for a very long time I had thought there was something wrong with me. This gave me a completely different way of viewing myself. I was not defective. I was quite simply being who I was supposed to be. Finally, it all made sense.

I felt discontent on the beach that day because I was not finished with my journey. In fact, I was just beginning the next phase. I now know that's the feeling that precedes the next leap forward. You see, there were many things I still needed to do. But now, instead of fitting somebody else's definition of who I needed to be, I needed to fit my own… or else I would never feel content.

by Jolene Morse

The last four years have seen me step outside of my comfort zone in many ways and in different capacities. But the two major outcomes have all been the same regardless of the result of the experience.

1. Every experience has taught me something
2. I have grown as an individual because I have stepped outside my comfort zone.

We are all scared. We carry our fears with us every day. But those same fears keep up stuck in the same place. The fear will never go away. We need to answer this most basic of questions – are we going to let the fear control us or are we are going to control the fear?

For example, I still get very scared when I am going to get on a stage to speak. But I now make a conscious choice on how I deal with this fear. I prepare well, I undertake deep breathing, I know that I am human and accept I am very unlikely to get everything perfect 100% of the time.

A comfort zone is a beautiful place to transit. But it is just that, a stopover, not a destination. Therefore, you should not dwell there too long. Keep moving forward towards your dreams. If you find somewhere along the way that feels right, that's okay. But if you do not feel content and feel you have more to give, then it's a clear sign you should step outside your comfort zone and chase your dreams. At the end of the day, what is the worst that can happen?

I do not profess to have all the answers. However, the last four years have shown me that if you can understand who you are and accept yourself for all your unique attributes then you can grow through taking true risk-based decisions rather than fear-based decisions.

by Jolene Morse

I am a mother, a risk professional, a board member, an educator, a writer, a children's author, and a public speaker. Most importantly, I am who I am supposed to be.

My journey does not end here. There is still more to do. Whilst the path I started on has fundamentally changed the way I view the world, I know now I have a deeper purpose to be part of a bigger, positive change for the world and for me this is only the beginning.

I cannot wait to see what comes next.

ABOUT THE AUTHOR

Sheetal **Pillai**

With an illustrious career of 20+ years in creative advertising and event management at Option 1 Live, Sheetal is now the COO of Option 1 Design Studio Australasia.

Sheetal's an exemplar of visionary leadership and entrepreneurial prowess, especially in immersive tech and content fusion. She's fostered meaningful connections across Asia and the East, driven by her creative ingenuity.

Sheetal's mentorship and coaching are pivotal, focusing on empowering individuals, particularly women professionals.

Her unwavering guidance fuels their remarkable journeys. Noteworthy is her influential role on SAE UAE's advisory board, shaping courses and nurturing student career paths.

With an unwavering passion for strategic planning and impactful communication, Sheetal's influence

ABOUT THE AUTHOR

is far-reaching across diverse sectors. Her impact extends to the wellness and fitness domain, creating an indelible legacy there as well.

Instagram	instagram.com/pillai.sheetal
LinkedIn	linkedin.com/in/sheetalpillaii

by Sheetal Pillai

Triumph of the Soul:
A Journey of Resilience and Empowerment

In the misty dawn of 1998, I embarked on a professional odyssey as a graphic designer in a distinguished government firm nestled in the heart of Abu Dhabi, UAE. Fueled by a spark of ambition that danced within me, I charted a course of self-study, buoyed by the invaluable guidance of my colleagues and mentors. Simultaneously, I immersed myself in a sea of online tutorials, a lifeline that sustained me as I pursued the elusive treasure of a coveted bachelor's degree.

Little did I fathom the profound impact this humble genesis would have, kindling an inferno within my soul that would lead to an extraordinary voyage of self-discovery and personal metamorphosis. Though I initially embarked on the path of a graphic designer to garner financial support for my pursuit of a specialized Bachelor's degree in Computer Science with a focus on Forensic Sciences at the mountain state university of West Virginia, destiny had other designs for me.

by Sheetal Pillai

Having undergone rigorous training under the esteemed Forensic and Telecommunication Authority of the United Arab Emirates, my intention was to forge a career within the esteemed ranks of the Dubai Police Force. Little did I anticipate that my part-time employment as a graphic designer would act as a catalyst, unlocking a wellspring of artistic inspiration that propelled me towards extraordinary realms.

The fusion of creativity and technological prowess infused my endeavors with an unyielding passion, guiding me to awe-inspiring places where imagination knows no boundaries. With each stroke of my brush and every pixel I manipulated, I discovered new horizons that beckoned me towards uncharted territories.

Thus, from the embryonic stages of my career as a graphic designer, borne out of a need for financial stability, emerged a kaleidoscope of transformative experiences. I am forever grateful for the opportunities that have shaped my destiny.

In the depths of my exploration into my career and future, I found myself diving headfirst into the tumultuous waters of matrimony at the tender age of 19. Yes, 19. This colossal shift in direction at such a young and vulnerable stage engulfed me in a swirling tempest of uncertainty. Self-doubt became my constant companion as I embarked on a treacherous journey, striving to navigate the treacherous currents of work, studies, and the immense weight of marital responsibilities.

Both my husband and I were on the precipice of our career paths, grappling with the intricacies of financial stability. This fragile tightrope act left me teetering on the edge of insecurity, questioning my ability to support him and questioning my own readiness to shoulder such adult burdens. My youthful inexperience whispered doubts, casting shadows

by Sheetal Pillai

upon my decision-making abilities. The weight of these uncertainties grew heavier, exacerbated by the suffocating presence of living in a joint family that offered no solace or guidance.

In the confines of my isolated existence, shielded from the outside world, my fragile sense of self began to crumble. I lost sight of my own dreams and personal growth, consumed by the responsibilities of building a family. The dependency that grew within me eroded my sense of identity, leaving me adrift in a sea of doubts and insecurities.

Despite my ex-husband's efforts to understand my struggles and provide support, the gaping chasm between our thoughts and aspirations widened. At first, I failed to recognize the signs, overshadowed by my youth and inexperience. Looking back now, I realize the disparity between us, with him being six years my senior, weighed heavily on our relationship. While we shared a cordial friendship, as a couple, we stood as polar opposites, drifting further apart with each passing day.

This divide grew more pronounced after the birth of our son, who became the guiding star of my life. Two years into parenthood, we made the difficult decision to part ways amicably, aiming to provide our child with a loving and stable environment. The path of separation was not without its hardships, as it shattered the peace within our family and brought forth tragedy in their eyes. Coming from a spiritual Indian family background, where divorce or separation were unfathomable concepts, my journey was met with disbelief and disruption.

Amidst the heavy burden of expectations and the relentless pursuit of appeasing everyone, I found myself facing an arduous task. Yet, in the midst of this overwhelming turmoil, my parents emerged as steadfast pillars of unwavering support, providing

by Sheetal Pillai

strength and solace during the darkest moments. Their unwavering presence by my side, despite their own doubts and concerns about societal judgment and the impact on my younger siblings, became a source of immense comfort.

My mother, a woman of extraordinary fortitude, became my rock, shouldering my burdens with a quiet grace, shedding silent tears when no one else was watching. Her indomitable spirit and unwavering love served as a guiding light in my life, an exemplar of resilience in the face of adversity. She is my idol, my beacon of strength and unwavering determination.

In moments of doubt and struggle, I draw strength from her unwavering presence, knowing that she will always be there to catch me when I stumble. In a world fraught with challenges, she remains my role model, a source of hope and inspiration that empowers me to weather every storm that comes my way.

Moreover, my younger sister, who should have been the one seeking support, became my source of strength. With maturity beyond her years, she comforted and encouraged me, offering the moral support I needed to stay strong and forge ahead. I learned valuable lessons from her strong-headedness and unwavering support, turning to her as another pillar of strength in my life.

In the tapestry of life, it is the love and support of family that helps us navigate through the darkest moments. My parents and sister have been my rock, my guiding stars, and my inspiration to keep moving forward, regardless of the challenges that lay ahead.

Amidst the shattering aftermath of a failed marriage and the relentless judgments of society, the weight of single motherhood descended upon me, enveloping my soul with an overwhelming sense of uncertainty. Questions haunted my every waking moment: "How will I provide my son with a good life? What if I

by Sheetal Pillai

stumble and fail? What if he looks back and tells me I'm not a good mother?" The echoes of self-doubt reverberated within, threatening to dismantle my fragile resolve.

Yet, as the shadows of doubt began to dissipate, the light of my education and life experiences started to shimmer and glow. It had been an arduous journey, one fraught with anxiety attacks and bouts of depression. But for the sake of my precious son, I made a resolute decision to gather the fragmented pieces of my life and forge ahead.

I tirelessly took on multiple jobs, dedicating my time to securing our financial stability. Though this left me with less time to spend with my son, I was fortunate to find an exceptional caretaker who helped me manage the affairs of our home, allowing me to concentrate on putting food on the table. I assumed the role of the provider, mustering strength from the depths of my being, and gradually, I built the courage to establish a small, homegrown design agency called Depingere alongside my job as a 3D designer.

Amidst the delicate balancing act of tending to my son's needs and nurturing my fledgling career, vulnerability became my constant companion. Yet, they say that women possess an inherent strength, and in my case, every passing moment seemed to imbue me with greater resilience and unwavering confidence. Despite the challenges, my son never uttered a complaint. He busied himself with toys, friends, and schoolwork, always greeting me with open arms and an infectious smile upon my return home.

In the intricate maze of life's challenges, two extraordinary friends, Janet and Jaina, emerged as beacons of light, guiding my way through the darkest uncertainties. Their unwavering belief in my abilities and the inspiring talks they shared became my lifeline,

by Sheetal Pillai

lifting my spirit when doubt threatened to overwhelm me. In moments of despair, the comforting embrace of steadfast friends can rekindle a spark of hope, reminding us of the immense strength and untapped potential within. Shubs, another dear friend, deserves special mention for being my pillar of support during my weakest moments, using her wit and humor to brighten my days and teaching me to find joy and fun even amidst adversity.

Amidst a tapestry of personal growth and aspirations, the world plunged into the darkness of an unfortunate recession. The company I poured my heart into shuttered its doors, leaving many of us without salaries for months. In the face of adversity, I clung to the belief that closed doors pave the way for new beginnings. It was during this tumultuous time that my agency, now transformed from Depingere to Option 1 Live, became my beacon of light. With a colleague turned partner, we embarked on a daring new venture, intertwining creativity, technology, and events, bravely unlocking new doors of opportunity.

Hand in hand, we toiled day and night, nurturing our brand and metamorphosing a modest two-person venture into a flourishing global entity, with branches stretching across continents. My partner and a mentor, shone brightly as my guiding star in a male-dominated industry. Amidst the challenges of being the only woman, his unwavering support and belief in my abilities fueled my determination to carve out my unique identity. I am forever indebted for his constant presence and unwavering faith in me.

In our journey to run the company, we faced a symphony of triumphs and tribulations. Countless obstacles tempted us to surrender, but our indomitable spirits refused to yield. The recession sent waves of uncertainty, and our path was paved with rejections and financial instability. Traveling

by Sheetal Pillai

via public transport, cutting expenses to the bone, we clung to the belief that we would make it happen.

In the early days, a shared coworking space became our sanctuary, lacking the means for a dedicated office or full-time staff. But as we secured our first client through a pivotal connection, a glimmer of hope emerged. Embracing growth, we secured an office space and appointed a small but dedicated team. From there, our trajectory soared, etching our story into the annals of history.

Yet, as our business flourished, so did the burdens of stress. The stress of growth and transformation tested our resilience, serving as a testament to the transformative journey we had embarked upon. Today, we stand resolute and proud, weathering the storms, emerging stronger than ever before. From humble beginnings to an empire with 500+ clients, I stand tall as a resilient leader in a man's world.

Amidst the extraordinary journey, I battled with inner demons that threatened to engulf my spirit. The weight of depression, anxiety attacks, insomnia, and self-inflicted torment cast shadows over my existence. In search of solace, I encountered enigmatic healers and psychologists who delved deep into the recesses of my soul. Among them, Meetu Singh, a healing therapist, wove a potent tapestry of sound healing, becoming my dearest confidant and guiding light with her profound wisdom. She remains the one I turn to in times of need, my closest friend and staunchest well-wisher. Embracing vulnerability and shedding shame, I learned that each trial was a doorway to profound personal growth and self-discovery.

In a world where mental health issues are shrouded in taboo, especially for women, I discovered a sanctuary of support and enlightenment in the presence of my cherished friends, Kim and Reshmi.

by Sheetal Pillai

They guided me towards the transformative power of self-love and self-reliance, illuminating the path to healing and self-discovery. Embracing healing modalities like yoga and meditation, I delved into the depths of a healthy mind and body, finding solace in the ethereal energy of Kim's crystals during meditation, offering me a profound sense of healing on a subconscious level.

In a society that is still hesitant to fully embrace these practices, I unearthed a profound truth – the human mind possesses an innate power of healing. Empowered by the profound wisdom gleaned from books like "Ikigai" and "Conversations with God," I realized that our minds hold the key to unlocking transformative healing potential. Drawing inspiration and motivation from the lives of remarkable individuals such as Oprah Winfrey, Steve Jobs, Nelson Mandela, Shaolin Master, and Sadhguru, I found their impactful videos to be a guiding light during moments of despair and demotivation, lifting me towards greater heights of personal growth and transformation.

Throughout my journey, I have been truly blessed to encounter extraordinary souls who left an indelible impact as friends, always there when I needed them the most. Their unwavering support and presence became the foundation upon which I built my resilience and determination to navigate life's challenges with renewed strength and hope.

From each trial, I emerged like a phoenix, radiant and triumphant, rising from the ashes. Option 1 Group of Companies transformed into an empire, spanning continents and offering cutting-edge events, groundbreaking technology, and immersive digital experiences. What started as a single department bloomed into a diverse array of divisions, encompassing research in technology,

by Sheetal Pillai

content development including stunning animations and captivating drone shots, and ingenious SAAS solutions. As I nurtured my team, I witnessed their remarkable growth and witnessed them creating marvels alongside the company. The dedication of my staff, for which I am forever grateful, propelled me into the limelight as an advocate for women's leadership, a member of advisory boards, a mentor, and a leadership coach. A leader's strength lies in empowering and trusting their team, for it is they who work wonders and elevate the company to new heights.

As my passion for entrepreneurship soared, I set my sights on a new venture into the enchanting land of Australia as Option 1 Design Studio PTY LTD. A celebration of unwavering dedication, this endeavor embraced the fusion of technology and content, a testament to my entrepreneurial prowess. In this dramatic tale of triumph and resilience, my spirit soared, forever reaching for the stars. An entity encouraging all women to explore the technical aspect within them.

To the women who dare to dream, I extend an unwavering message of hope and resilience. Amidst life's tempestuous seas, never surrender, for greatness lies within your grasp. With unwavering determination and unwavering perseverance, embark on a journey that defies expectations and soars beyond limits. My voyage stands as a testament to the indomitable spirit of womanhood—an unwavering belief that we possess the strength to conquer any adversity. Together, let us ignite the sparks of empowerment, nurturing a legacy of female leadership that knows no boundaries.

As I gaze upon the tapestry of my life, I stand proudly before the legacy I have built. From the crucible of self-doubt, I have emerged as a warrior—an architect

by Sheetal Pillai

of dreams, a mentor, and an unwavering champion of women's empowerment. In this epoch of existence, I am resolute in my endeavor to leave an indelible imprint upon the world—a testament to the enduring power that resides within every woman. It is my fervent hope that my journey becomes a guiding star, illuminating the path for women across the globe, inspiring them to rise above the ashes of adversity, embrace the fires within their souls, and forge their own triumphant destinies.

ABOUT THE AUTHOR

Clare Jobson

Hello I am Clare Jobson and I'm originally from Adelaide. I have a diverse background, which includes transitioning from my prior nursing career to becoming a lawyer later in life. I now specialise in family law and parenting coordination.

Travelling around Australia as a Defence spouse, I have practiced in the Northern Territory, New South Wales, South Australia and Queensland. I have worked for Government, the Community legal sector and in private practice, prior to opening my own firm CJ Legal in 2015.

I didn't feel like I belonged as a lawyer after I first graduated, because my nursing background provided me with a different perspective, but I am now actively leaning into all of my skills which enable me to provide holistic support to the parents and families I work with. I am proud that I am diverse and view life through a different lens. I am passionate about kindness and meeting humans where we find them. I apply a trauma informed approach to my work and am in the process of writing a book to provide parents with insight into how it feels to be children of separation sharing the experiences of the now adults I have interviewed so far. I intend to draw on both my nursing and legal backgrounds to tell their stories.

I have appeared on the Happy Lawyer Happy Life Podcast (episode 121) and the Military Wife Military Life Podcast (episode 49). I have contributed to Lawyer's weekly articles and can be found on the College of Law Admission to practice Academy 2020 "Coming to Law later in life" online panel recording.

When I am not at work, I enjoy spending time with my partner Jason and our furbabies and being involved with the Marilyn Jetty Swim based in Adelaide fundraising for Cancer Council SA.

LinkedIn	linkedin.com/in/clare-jobson-59052765
Instagram	instagram.com/jobsonclare
Bus. Facebook	facebook.com/CJLegalAust
Bus. Website	CJ Legal www.cjlegal.net.au
Also on websites	Parenting Coordination Australia https://parentingcoordinationaustralia.com.au/find-parenting-coordinator
	Resolution SA https://resolutionsa.net.au/our-members
	Australian Association of Collaborative Professionals https://www.collaborativeaustralia.com.au/find-a-professional/user/314
	International Academy of Collaborative Professionals https://www.collaborativepractice.com/members/21546
	Resolution Institute https://resolution.institute/publicprofile?ContactKey=9DF4DA7B-3960-4768-8914-FA857FFA3D6F

by Clare Jobson

From Grief to Growth
(Empathy my superpower ... and my curse)

Grief is a difficult thing to start my story with. I acknowledge that most people associate grief with the loss of a loved one. Yet grief also strikes with other major losses in our lives, and often we are not prepared...

I was sitting in a very grey, bland waiting area of the Intensive Care Unit at the Royal Adelaide Hospital. Not because I was waiting to visit someone, but because my ex-husband had gone in to see the Nursing Unit Manager of the ICU looking for work. At that time, we had not long returned from living and working as nurses in London for the best part of two and a half years. It was a long time ago now, over 22 years.

As I sat there with my sunglasses on, pretending not to be taking up space, an older couple came out from ICU and sat directly across from me. They had both been reduced to tears and were comforting each other. I realised as I sat there with them, that my eyes had filled, and my vision was becoming blurry. And I couldn't stop myself. Tears were slowly and silently falling down my face behind the cover of my

by Clare Jobson

sunglasses because I could FEEL their overwhelming distress. I remember feeling so powerless to help them or offer any comfort which was difficult for me to sit with. I did not know them, or whom they had come to visit. It could have been their child, their grandchild or any other family member or friend. Who they were there to visit wasn't the reason for my silent sobbing. As an empath, I could feel radiating from them the news that they'd just received wasn't good. I knew in my heart they may have just said their final goodbyes to whomever their loved one was. I had no way of making it better for them. I had no way of fixing it. Empathy, you see, is both my superpower and my curse. They sat there for some time until they had finished crying and had composed themselves enough to take on the rest of their day. They took themselves away in the lift.

By the time my ex-husband and I were leaving, I too had composed myself again. It's strange... I don't think I've actually shared my entire feelings about this moment, until writing this right now. I didn't realise it at the time I was sitting there, as I do now upon reflection (which I've not ever been great at doing), but I was suffering from empathy and compassion overload. That couple were grieving their sad news and I was, unknown to me at that time, grieving the future loss of what I had always thought to be my "calling in life". I remember thinking, if I couldn't hold myself together in that situation and be able to help people, how could I possibly return to my own nursing career in a hospital environment and provide care to people without falling apart every, single, day. That moment created the seed that took root and grew into my decision to eventually leave nursing, my calling. It didn't happen straight away, of course. Some time and considerable pondering and planning were needed.

by Clare Jobson

Not too long after that pivotal day, I discovered an ad in the paper to study law in Darwin, you know back in the days when we looked at our news in hardcopy instead of via social media. I recall that I had made an extremely flippant comment to my ex-husband along the lines of, "How would you feel about moving to Darwin?" I later found myself applying and then, to my total amazement, actually being accepted to study in law in Darwin. (Insert nervous giggle here.) You see, I, who had not completed year 12 and was a hospital trained nurse, had been accepted for a place at university. But not just law, oh no. I had decided to do a dual degree in Law and Information Technology because, I thought, as a mature age student I needed to do much more than just one thing to get anywhere. The rest, as they say, is history.

As an Adelaide girl in a working-class family with three brothers, two older and one younger, I had always wanted to be a nurse from a very young age and had not contemplated that a day would ever come when I didn't want to be a nurse anymore. I saw it as a calling you see, and I had dedicated my life up until that point to caring for those in hospital and health environments in Australia and the UK. The majority of my nursing career was caring for children and babies, though I had some patches of caring for adults too.

Not only did I believe nursing to be a calling, I believed it to be a privilege. As a nurse, I was with people in their best and worst life moments, from birth through to death. Paradoxically, the lens through which I had experienced these life and death moments was not always on my best days. You see, my nursing career had exposed me to some extremely traumatic events, especially for little people, some of which were entirely preventable...

by Clare Jobson

I can recall one young girl in particular. I will call her Nikki. Nikki was around 10-years old when she arrived on the ward. She had developed some troubling and unexplained physical symptoms in her legs. She had constant leg pain, trouble walking and was very unsteady when she did try to walk unaided. Nikki went through extensive testing by the medical staff who were unable to identify any developmental or mechanical causes of her problem.

The discovery of no known physical explanation for her issue led to Nikki being referred to the mental health team who worked with her extensively. They discovered she had once been a passionate, budding ballet dancer. They also discovered the catalyst for Nikki's leg problems was her parents separating when she was about 8-years old. Ballet, which was once a place of passion and absolute enjoyment for her, had turned sour and had become the battlefield on which her parents spent endless time arguing with each other. The problems with her legs didn't happen straight away. In fact, it had been a slow deterioration over a period of about 18 months, which contributed to being difficult to establish the cause. As it turned out, it was the only thing Nikki had control over with her parents constant fighting and was her trauma response to being caught in the middle of it. When the cause was identified, the family was referred on for appropriate assistance in working through Nikki's issues and she was eventually discharged and walked out of the hospital without assistance or pain.

Sadly, I would be lying to you if I said Nikki's situation was unique. Yet I also acknowledge the tainted view my many years as a nurse had given me. I remember at one stage thinking to myself, if I rescued every child from the difficult situation they were in, I could not move in my own home.

by Clare Jobson

When I made the decision to study law in Darwin, I intentionally set out to avoid areas where I was required to tap into any empathy and compassion. As described, I had become burnt out by the trauma I had been exposed to. In addition to my workplace trauma, I had also supported one of my brothers through his marriage breakdown and family court experience with ongoing parenting conflict. I had endured my painful journey with infertility which was diagnosed at the tender age of 22 whilst working with children and caring for children of family and friends. Later in my life, I had my own turbulent marriage and failed IVF attempt. That happened only a couple of years prior to running away overseas to live in London. Running away from those things only delayed the inevitable. It was to transpire, that at the beginning of my fourth year at university after returning to Australia, I would go through my own separation and subsequent divorce.

I had no plans to work in family law. In fact, at the commencement of my legal studies I actively chose elective units of a commercial nature. I had decided at one stage that if I did work at all with family law matters, I would only work as an Independent Children's Lawyer (not realising at that time of being a law student, that a solicitor must have a minimum of 5 years family law experience working with parties, before being able to do the ICL course).

My life has been very much what I describe as a choose your own adventure novel, the kind I used to enjoy reading as a child. With everything life has thrown my way I've just thought, oh Ok let's do this now instead and tried to make the most of it on the way. I have always been a "soldier on", "one foot in front of the other", "head down and bum up" type of person.

by Clare Jobson

I met my partner, Jason, in Darwin at the end of that messy year of separation. As he is a defence member, my life then took on the unique challenges associated with moving every few years to a new place with each posting. If I am honest, defence life is not easy for families and partners. However, moving around every few years has meant I have met some wonderful people along the way. I have always felt like I am blessed in some ways because I get to take pieces of those I've met with me and leave some pieces of myself behind for when we shall see each other again.

Our first posting together meant I found myself in Sydney as a baby lawyer in the Community Legal Centre (CLC) sector. It was during my time in this sector that I was first exposed to working with people embarking on their own navigation of the family law system.

We moved to NSW during the post global financial crisis era. At that time, there was no paid work for lawyers, and I was competing for work with lawyers who had studied in NSW, so... I was just the unknown outsider from Darwin. I found myself relying on my nursing background for income at a well-baby unit and initially worked as a volunteer solicitor. I also decided it was a good idea to enrol myself in a Masters of Family Law and a Masters of Commercial Litigation to keep my skills alive and my brain active. A dual masters was not particularly compatible with my recently diagnosed (at that time) rheumatoid arthritis, so I had to cut back my study load due to my health.

The Principal Solicitor of the first CLC in NSW where I volunteered for two nights per week made arrangements with his staff for them to all take their leave back-to-back. This meant he was able to offer me a short contract as a paid employee. As each person went on leave, I "hot desked" and was granted a supported and unique exposure to practice areas I had not previously worked in.

by Clare Jobson

By the time we said goodbye to Sydney, I had been employed in various roles between four different CLCs in NSW and had met some amazing and passionate solicitors dedicated to social justice. Around this time, I realised that, even though I had actively been avoiding it, my prior nursing skillset enabled me to view family law issues through a more holistic lens than traditionally trained solicitors who had been trained to just tackle the legal issues. I eventually realised that it was foolish not to draw on those skills to assist families with the best achievable and child-focussed outcomes.

Moving from Sydney to Adelaide was a strange posting experience as I had left Adelaide as a nurse and returned as a lawyer. This meant I was effectively becoming a stranger in my hometown and the small legal community there.

Defence life brings unique challenges because of a perception that you won't be around long. Accordingly, I was often overlooked for full-time roles. I worked at Public Trustee as an administrative officer until I was able to organise my paperwork to practice in South Australia. Each move interstate brought new and unique challenges due to each state-based law society requirements.

I eventually opened my own practice. CJ Legal was born in South Australia in June 2015 after a couple of years working between Public Trustee and a couple of private family lawyer firms in Adelaide. Not long after opening my own practice, I undertook the Independent Children's Lawyer training.

When Jason received his next posting order, the next challenge was moving CJ Legal from Adelaide to Brisbane. There was a bit more red tape than the usual with my own business, but... you do what you have to do.

by Clare Jobson

My time so far in Brisbane has been eventful. I have maintained my own practice, initially running it as an Adelaide business remotely from Brisbane, until the end of the 2019 financial year. This meant my Adelaide-based court matters required seeking leave to appear by telephone, flying down to appear, or briefing an agent or barrister to appear on my behalf. I was also initially working a 20-hour per week part-time contract at a local community legal service in addition to running my own practice.

The COVID pandemic threw everyone a huge curveball. However, it actually made my remote business easier to run. I guess I was a little ahead of my profession with methods I had adopted previously. My prior juggling had enabled me to be more resilient and I was able to assist other firms as a consultant during that time as we were able to appear in court via video conferencing. Not someone to sit ruminating too long, I also decided during COVID that it was an opportunity to undertake further training to improve my skills.

These days, I am collaboratively trained as a family lawyer, coach and in wills and estates. I am trained in high conflict and child inclusive mediation.

Additionally, I am a qualified parenting coordinator and am enthusiastically passionate about this role in particular. The reason is I feel I can now embrace empathy as more of a superpower than a curse as my prior nursing background compliments my ability to assist parents through parenting coordination.

Parenting coordination is not easy work. It requires working through difficult and often painful separations to assist parents to find and implement child-focussed solutions to their conflict. As difficult as it can be, it is very rewarding work and my hope is that by doing this work, there can be fewer Nikkis in hospital in the future.

by Clare Jobson

And finally, coming soon, is a book that has been on my "drawing-board" for some years now. It will assist parents navigating separation and those assisting parents navigating separation. In preparation for the book, I have interviewed adults who were children of divorced parents to obtain their insight and unique perspectives. In combination with my nursing and legal backgrounds, I am intending to provide a different lens to view parenting arrangements through.

Yes, grief is a challenging state. And though it stems from loss, any loss, it's amazing what it allows you to find... if you simply keep looking.

"True transformation means developing a wise and generous relationship with ourselves, not making ourselves something we are not. Even the best personal development strategies won't work if you're effectively trying to stick beautiful self-improvement wallpaper over your lumpy I-hate-myself walls."

Toni Knight

ABOUT THE AUTHOR

Toni Knight

Toni Knight is a psychotherapist and hypnotherapist who specialises in preventing and treating anxiety, trauma and burnout. Although based in Newcastle, NSW, Toni teaches and empowers people from all over Australia through her bespoke programs and workshops, both online and in person.

After earning her degree in psychology and spending many years using standard cognitive therapies, Toni's frustration with the slow pace of change led her to explore more effective ways to give people the practical tools and strategies that they need in order to achieve their goals and maintain their progress.

Toni is known for this very pragmatic approach, believing that a satisfying life is centred in flexibly living out your values, being able to use feelings as helpful signals, and optimising personal energy to enhance 'assertive living'.

ABOUT THE AUTHOR

She helps people to stop self-sabotage, knowing that this maddening tendency to shoot yourself in the foot will reduce when you are focused on what is helpful and consistently doing the simple things that align with who you really are and what you really want.

Toni is a self-described 'psychology nerd' who loves good coffee, her friends, beaches, and her husband, daughter, cat and dog. Toni describes them as the perfect team for living a vibrant, satisfying life.

Feel free to contact Toni by email and ask a question or just say hello!

Website: toniknight.co

Email: toni@toniknight.co

by Toni Knight

The ironic path beyond burnout

As a therapist I've learned, through humbly witnessing the journeys of thousands of women, that personal transformation isn't about self-improvement.

We don't need to improve ourselves. Instead, we need to become more of who we really are, without so much fear.

But nobody believes that. At least not at first.

Yet, as we free ourselves to safely connect with what truly matters to us and gives our life meaning, we can learn the skills needed to navigate the inner and outer barriers that have held us back.

Transformation is a journey of increasing self-acceptance, self-compassion and valued action because we are okay as we are.

We don't need to become more, but to let go of who we are not. And we are not our limiting beliefs, nor our bodies, feelings or actions.

True transformation means developing a wise and generous relationship with ourselves, not making *by Toni Knight*

ourselves something we are not. Even the best personal development strategies won't work if you're effectively trying to stick beautiful self-improvement wallpaper over your lumpy I-hate-myself walls.

And don't waste your time trying to fill that I'm-not-enough hole with more of... everything.

Those lumpy-bumpy bits of our inner and outer lives that we fear and despise are no more than stories. Stories that were once told to us, and that we now tell ourselves. Old, borrowed stories from people who didn't know any better.

Stories that have never been helpful, nor even true. Stories that can be changed.

Ironically, in reconnecting and living compassionately with themselves, many people experience a beautiful sense of more. No longer believing those false, limiting narratives about themselves, they free themselves to live powerfully according to their values and vision of a rich, meaningful life.

Self-recovery, not self-improvement. You don't need to be enhanced. You're not lacking.

Your compelling picture of a sweet, vibrant life may be the start of an important, transformative journey - one tiny step at a time, having fun, and starting today.

The journey out of burnout illustrates this idea perfectly.

My client Sue was a skilled administrator who led a support team for a large occupational therapy practice. But on day one at my office, Sue seemed little more than a remnant. She was exhausted and unwell - an unwell that can't be diagnosed, but that affected every aspect of her life. Her work, her marriage, her parenting, and her health were all suffering. She felt paralysed and blank. And the tears just wouldn't stop.

by Toni Knight

Sue, like so many of us, didn't know she was burning out until it almost devoured her. The more burnt out you are, the less awareness you can bring to how it's consuming you.

And burnout is surprisingly easy to ignore - until you can't. It's the new 'normal.'

It's almost inevitable when working in a society that worships productivity and is gamified for achievement.

So, we wage war on idleness and underachievement. We slay the to-do list, rescue the client in distress, rise up to higher levels with harder missions, forge ahead in bonded teams of comrades, collect rewards and accumulate prestige, and battle our competitors.

The psychology of 'soldiering on', regardless, is baked into our working lives.

Sue's motivation to excel reflected her caring and commitment. And she learned her superpowers of empathy, duty, and loyalty early in life. Having a younger sister who was the 'preferred' child, Sue grew up striving to meet her parents' unreasonable expectations of her in exchange for rare glimpses of approval. Affection was in even shorter supply.

Sue learned early to be hypervigilant regarding signs of disapproval so that she could do even more to wrestle back some sense of being enough in her parents' eyes. Although Sue never experienced what she'd call 'trauma', her emotional needs - for love, acceptance, belonging, achievement and autonomy were all significantly neglected.

Childhood emotional abuse and neglect, often unrecognised even in adulthood, can sabotage our wellbeing with uncanny stealth. Until we identify and address its legacy, we assume that our problems are due instead to some fundamental brokenness or badness that resides in us - as if we are the problem.

by Toni Knight

As if we are not enough.

The resulting lack of self-compassion is heartbreaking to witness.

Sue came to understand that her early experiences taught her some unfortunate life lessons: that she is not safe to be herself and ask for what she wants, that she is unworthy of love, approval or freedom unless she earns it, and that she is not capable of being something other than what her parents deemed her to be.

Our life lessons are subconsciously filed away. We continue to use these learnings as a frame through which we notice and interpret our world long after many of these learnings have stopped being useful, if they ever were.

Sue believed, for example, that in order for people to approve of her, she must fawn and be generous first. And the positive reactions she then experienced, as her life progressed, seemed to prove her correct.

A false veneer of 'truth' solidified many unhelpful beliefs for Sue.

Such beliefs cause us pain - emotional and sometimes physical. They drive self-sabotage and conflict behaviours.

Clusters of related beliefs, feelings and experiences form familiar states of being that when triggered, take over and sometimes drive our behaviour in unhelpful ways that diminish our experience of life. Some call these states our 'ego-parts'.

One of Sue's 'parts' is a harsh self-critic. That part of Sue has learned that it's safest to shame her into paying attention to all her mistakes and potential mistakes, so that she can correct them before someone else notices her inadequacy.

by Toni Knight

We all have ego-parts that are activated when triggered. Some of our parts are very useful, even fun. But like Sue, we all have parts that formed early in life and still carry childlike beliefs about ourselves and our world. Those parts are out of touch with the maturity of our current life stage. When triggered, those parts can make us suddenly feel like a child - very hurt, scared, guilty or angry.

Sue could hear the childlike nature of some of her unhelpful parts when she gave them a voice in our sessions. One little voice told of Sue's need to shut up and not say anything, in case she gets in trouble. She could hear the naive logic that is typical of the young age when these learnings first occurred.

Sue likened these limiting beliefs to a spiritual injury - an incapacity to realise all she could be and live an abundant, values-centred, fulfilling life according to her own priorities.

Ironically, this made her the ideal employee.

And Sue was a beloved employee. She consistently put in 50-hour weeks, having precious little left for her family at the far end of the day.

There was still the housework. She had no time to exercise, socialise or stabilise. Through her work, Sue was able to receive what her parts craved - respect, achievement, belonging and worth. Conditional on performing, of course.

It wasn't a great bargain, but one that Sue unconsciously embraced.

Many women have parts that tell stories similar to Sue's.

These parts drive unhelpful behaviours such as always saying yes to requests; having rigidly perfectionistic standards; self-silencing through a fear of expressing opinions or asking for what we

by Toni Knight

want or need; excessive responsibility for the success and functioning of other people and processes; making self-care conditional on first achieving goals (regardless of our actual needs); and being harshly self-critical when we inevitably start to wither and drop some of the many balls we are juggling.

These behaviours generate, and are in turn strengthened by, anxiety, insecurity, resentment, pessimism, and low self-worth in a vicious cycle that pulls us into despair.

Yet these same characteristics, when applied modestly in the right contexts, make women powerful - powerful parents, partners, leaders, healers, helpers, and teachers. We bearers of these characteristics are highly empathetic, agreeable, cooperative, and conscientious.

It's the rigid, pervasive use of these strategies across all contexts all the time that makes them problematic.

When we succumb to the larger forces that undermine our wellbeing and deny us our personal rights, we become tired and resentful. We burn out.

But we don't always have to say yes or complete something to a high standard. We can look after ourselves and achieve. We can speak up. We can criticise our strategy without being hard on ourselves.

When we free ourselves, even somewhat from the riptide of burnout, we can rescue enough presence to see what our ego-parts are doing - scaring us into believing that claiming autonomy and making healthy choices is a bad risk.

Sue was so burnt out that she had to risk changing the way she did work and non-work life. Her health was failing, and she was sliding into depression.

Sue learned how to stop struggling and instead, communicate with the childlike parts that were

by Toni Knight

afraid for her to take responsibility for flexible health decisions. We validated the early learning of those parts (they did a good job of protecting Sue in her early years), told those parts the truth of Sue's current abilities, and asked them gently to relax and allow Sue to make decisions as the mature woman she is now.

Let those childlike parts be your life passengers, as long as they don't drive your bus. And when they try to take the wheel, have that chat again, as a kind parent to a frightened child. Then, take action from the mature parts that connect you with your values.

Sue was developing a healthy relationship with herself, based on acceptance, compassion and wisdom.

She undertook some activities to discover and reconnect with her values, followed by an 'energy audit' - noting all the activities that left her feeling drained, disappointed, resentful, or stressed. Sue then crafted her job gradually to reduce that list of energy zappers, first by reducing her work hours and then starting to say a kind 'no' to her colleagues when they made additional requests of her.

Your energy is your gold. Invest it wisely. The things that matter to you may not always involve pleasant activities, but by definition, they will be worth the investment of your precious energy. Let go of the rest.

Sue was taking values-centred action. Back to the gym and getting help at home. Progress was mixed, as expected, and sometimes her parts screamed that she was in danger. But Sue wisely persisted in the face of those fearful feelings, born of childlike beliefs. She told her parts she was safe, and that they could let her, the wise adult, protect them.

Feelings are signals about things that matter to us. It's good to get curious about them. Sometimes, though, our feelings arise from those old unhelpful stories

by Toni Knight

inside us, rather than the more helpful stories that allow us to skilfully navigate our terrain.

Like a false fire alarm, our feelings are real, but there's no actual fire. When your internal alarm goes off without a valid cause, address your over-reactive fire alarm itself.

Sue was able to connect with her powerful parts, those learnings that reminded her of her successes, strengths, and values. In this state, Sue knew she could succeed if she took steps that made her uncomfortable, but not terrified.

Time then to create fertile soil that supported her new 'fragile seedling' habits. Some people will be supportive - Sue's husband and daughters were great cheerleaders, even if they sometimes let her down. And some people may try to undermine her improvements, in order to restore the status quo.

That's what Sue's boss did. The healthier work hours and the saner workload was restoring Sue's vitality, day by day. Yet this positive redirection of Sue's energy was costing hours on the job and her boss would not accept this.

Sue's boss needed another insecure Sue to replace this person who had embraced an accepting, compassionate relationship with herself. This courageous woman put herself back in charge of her life, instead of being driven to burnout by those internal parts that demanded habitual servanthood to keep her emotionally 'safe'.

Sue reluctantly left for a position that supports the healthy person she is now. She didn't allow her massive investment in her work prevent her from starting again elsewhere.

When we last spoke, Sue was happy and well.

by Toni Knight

Too few employers are willing to pay for a steadfast and visionary investment in their people's wellbeing. We self-employed folk are equally ambivalent about the cost of investing in ourselves, acknowledging the benefits, yet delaying the hard decisions in the hope that it will somehow be easier later, perhaps after that next big thing. Perhaps.

We can't wait for that change of heart from our leaders. Although there are powerful cultural, political, and structural forces that drive burnout, we can, and must, halt the burnout trajectory within ourselves and among our peers.

We can build small communities of wellness. Resilience is a team sport.

But start now - the longer you wait, the longer it takes to recover.

Halting burnout starts with knowing the potential price of prioritising your wellness - promotions? pay? kudos?

Yet like any great investment, the benefits far outweigh the costs. What investment is more valuable than your health?

Within your team or community you can give your colleagues permission to check your okayness; all commit together to limit your work hours; all agree to safely say no if a request is too much; innovate together with your employer to implement healthy improvements in systems of work and resources; refuse to transmit cynicism and all call out, and stamp out incivility, exclusion, discrimination, aggression, prejudice, isolation and unfairness.

Overcoming burnout starts and finishes within relationships.

And your first relationship is with yourself. When you make peace with the many parts of yourself, you

by Toni Knight

open the door to personal transformation, and that empowers you to safely prioritise your wellness as a countercultural vote for yourself.

Within your teams you can mutually strengthen both health and excellence by nurturing a culture of 'wellness first'.

It's possible - Sue and many others have done it. You can become a wisely rebellious, transformed woman, and join the many of us who actively value our collective thriving.

ABOUT THE AUTHOR

Leonie Noble

Hi my name is Leonie and I am a proud seafood woman living in a large regional town in Western Australia and part time on a remote windswept limestone rock 55 kilometres off the midwest coast.

I have three amazing daughters and two beautiful grandchildren who light up my world. and a family that always support and challenge each other what could be better.

I wasnt sure what I should write to introduce myself but my life has been moulded by amazing strong women, grand mothers, aunts, and especially my mother who all made the lives around them better and worked so hard for their communities and families and who if born in a different time would have changed the world for the better.

It made me want to make my daughters lives one with memories that bring a smile at unexpected times and

ABOUT THE AUTHOR

hopefully the work that I have been fortunate to be involved in made a difference to another women. so that was a good start I thought.

Memories, good memories are what makes the hard times easier, the memory of being in a dinghy squid fishing with my three girls laughing like lunatics as we got covered by ink that dripped from our hair onto our faces, covered our clothes and stained our skin was for me in that moment magical and for a moment in time life was perfect. Perfect moments are worth reliving over and over and it doesnt matter where I am or what I am doing those perfect moments make me smile.

I have been fortunate to be able to work in areas that allowed me to engage with humans that make a difference who spend their lives fighting for a better world, a more equal and visible world where all voices are heard and valued and I thank those strong resilient women in my life both now and then who continue to inspire me to be better do better and try harder.

I hope you enjoy my story.
Take care,
Leonie

LinkedIn / linkedin.com/in/leonie-noble-98584231

by Leonie Noble

From boat to Boardroom

Growing up, my incredibly supportive mother always told me I learned to argue before I could talk. And what did I argue about? Everything! But she wanted me to learn to argue in favour of the greater good; not just to get my own way. So, fighting for the underdog became my cause. And while that was my mother's concern, my grandmother always said I was never going to fit into society's expectations of what women should think and do, so I shouldn't waste my time trying.

Yes, these two wonderful women had me pegged early as those two observations have largely defined the direction my life has taken.

However, for a while (quite a while, in fact) I was happy to be a stay-at-home mum with my three amazing daughters. You see, I had married into a rock lobster fishing family working off the mid-west coast of WA. The Abrolhos Islands are a cluster of small rock islands 55kms off Geraldton. The archipelago is not made up of tropical islands with white sand and palm trees as you might see in a holiday brochure.

by Leonie Noble

Instead, they are a windswept, barren, low-lying rock or shale island group mostly with limited telecommunications and emergency services. That said, it is the most starkly beautiful place I have ever had the fortune to live and work in. While there, I thought my life was idyllic. After all, even though it was heavily male dominated, I was able to live and spend time with my daughters and husband in an amazing and remote place. How lucky was I?

One day, a letter from the then Minister of Fisheries arrived. It outlined a slew of new legislation that would impact the fishing community at the Abrolhos Islands.

That letter flicked a switch in me, I knew it was never going to be enough to just enjoy the luxury of being a mother and wife anymore.

You see, the contents of that letter threatened the lifestyle of my family's my fellow islanders.' It represented an injustice to the industry and community we created and belonged to. Yes, that letter changed the direction of my life. After reading it... I was angry! There was no consultation process, no opportunity to provide input and no common courtesy or human decency. Instead, there was a plan that would adversely affect our livelihood and community.

So along with my neighbour and best friend, Natasha Colliver, we walked around our island. Yes, I know... there goes 15 minutes. (It really is that small!) But this was no relaxing stroll. We were organising. That night, we had a strategy meeting with six women around my kitchen table. We started a group called, Friends of the Abrolhos. At the end of that meeting, we knew the politicians were going to have to listen.

We wrote to every politician we could think of. We got on every government mailing list. We wrote submissions on everything to do with the Abrolhos.

by Leonie Noble

We invited the minister to come and talk to us. Yep... we made the type of noise politicians had to take notice of. As a group, Friends of the Abrolhos went on to raise money to ensure we had access to an emergency helicopter service and had a semblance of reasonable telecommunication service. And we didn't stop there. We got pretty much anything and everything that made our community a functioning one in the 21stt century.

When I stepped down as President, we had grown to over 150 members who came from many walks of life. Our concerted and unrelenting campaign led to changes in government consultation processes and created many opportunities for input into policy surrounding the Abrolhos. We had become the voice for the community and the area. It was a case of Power to the People, as we had become what politicians fear most... an organised and unified voice.

I could not have done this without support. Revolutions need helpers just as everyone needs their tribe. No, not a group of *yes-people*, but a group of like-minded people with the ability to work together for a common cause and who are confident in speaking their mind and being able to agree to disagree at times and move on with the majority. It was incredibly fortunate that we had that. And not just in the early days. I continue to have the support of amazing people around the work I do. That's what makes a difference. They help you understand failures are merely a stepping-stone to success which can be fixed next time around. Importantly, they lift you up and stop you from giving up.

After I stepped away from Friends of the Abrolhos the then Minister for Fisheries, Kim Chance, rang me and told me IF I wanted to continue to make a difference and influence government, it was time to put my money where my mouth was. What did that mean? It meant he appointed me to both the Abrolhos

by Leonie Noble

Islands Management Advisory Council (the board that dealt with everything close to my heart, so I thrived here) and I was the A-Zone representative on RLIAC, the rock lobster ministerial advisory council. (Not quite as much thriving occurred on RLIAC. I was one of the first two women appointed to RLIAC and the first Industry women on the AIMAC.)

I would like to say that it was all lovely and smooth sailing but given what I've just told you, you can probably guess that's not how it went. In fact, the first words spoken to me were, "Are you here to make the coffee?" Regardless of those disconcerted traditional thinking men, there were a few board members that were extraordinary men and have become lifelong mentors and friends.

And that baptism of fire? It ensured I was never a token woman on any board.

The impact that we had as women on RLIAC was quite extraordinary. Instead of making decisions on a purely economic basis that was not equitable across all fishers much of the time, we created a social impact thought process where any and all decisions made were examined for their social impacts.

Then we got a curly one from the Minister...

He asked the board to produce a way forward involving a quota system. This was, quite possibly, the hardest period of my life. It also was the most defining. I was subjected to 18 months of death threats; my husband's fishing gear and boat were consistently vandalised, and we had to ban the children from answering the phone!

Being woken up at 2am to a voice telling me my daughter was looking beautiful, but she wouldn't be next time I saw her was terrifying. The upside was I found out just how strong I was. It solidified in me that we all needed to do better, to be better and to

by Leonie Noble

provide safe places while we changed the way the world was working.

After that experience, I needed to take a step back from the seafood industry. I needed time to enjoy being wife and mother for a while.

Yep... nice thought. You see, my need to do something meant taking a step back didn't last long because an opportunity arose that I couldn't say no to.

I was appointed to the Rural Regional and Remote (RRR) Network in WA, a government board providing direct input into government policy around issues like education, health, telecommunication, palliative care, childcare and the list goes on. The network also produced a quarterly magazine that showcased the women making our communities better places. It was incredibly fulfilling to be part of this cause.

I chaired that board for four years. During this time, I used my free time to start a university degree via correspondence. It wasn't always fun, so to get me through I started a diary in my early days there. It contained all the discriminatory remarks I had either heard or had been told. These usually made me laugh and refocus my thoughts. To this day, my favourite is, "Boards can't afford women directors because it was expensive to paint a boardroom pink."

For all my sins, I then took on the role of National President of Women in Seafood Australasia (WISA). For four years, I chaired WISA and enjoyed and continue to celebrate the women I worked alongside and met along the way.

My sole focus there was to increase the visibility of women in the seafood sector... and for a very good reason. In Australia, 55% of the wild catch, aquaculture, research and supply chain are women. Yet less than 6% of seafood women sit in management positions.

by Leonie Noble

So, we started working towards changing that because of a simple truth... if we are not visible, we are not in the mix. From this work, I have spent many years working with and mentoring seafood women across Australia and internationally. I love it. It's given me opportunities to speak at many conferences across the world and to learn about international seafood communities. I currently sit on both national and international seafood boards. The opportunities that have been available to this noisy girl from Geraldton still amaze me.

Through all this time, I was deputy or acting chair of the federal government's Regional Development Australia's Midwest Gascoyne board (RDAMWG). Additionally, I was on the 3-state Cross Jurisdictional Northern Alliance board. The understanding of regional development I have attained, has underpinned much of my work on all board or community projects because it deals with the hard truths of affordability and service provision. I stepped down from this board in 2019. I wanted to do more in my local community so needed to better balance of national and international work versus community work.

All these roles, and many others, led to being included in the Australian delegation to APEC's Women's Economic Forum held in Peru. What an amazing experience! Through this, I've had the opportunity to work with likeminded women globally, many of whom I have had the privilege of mentoring over the years. This has dramatically increased my knowledge of global policy development and funding. I have since returned to Peru and trekked from the bowels of the Amazon to the mountains of Bolivia. It was an amazing journey with beautiful people in a very special part of the world.

by Leonie Noble

Currently, I chair the National Rural Women's Coalition (NRWC). This is one of the six national women's boards funded by the federal government to provide advocacy and advice which feeds directly into government policy. The NRWC prides itself in the opportunities it provides to our rural, remote and regional women across Australia. We provide digital learnings that allow our women to learn from home so childcare and travel costs can be minimised while family responsibilities can be attended to.

We do this through webinars developed and delivered about topics such as succession planning, taxation, social media, mental health strategies, leadership, project management, networking and the list goes on. We also have a multiple award-winning signature residential program on leadership and advocacy held in Canberra each year.

As a seafood woman, the NRWC has been an interesting learning curve for me and has provided numerous opportunities to spread that knowledge. I've had the opportunity to educate a huge range of industries, government agencies and civil society both nationally and internationally. Everyone now knows the importance of officially recognising seafood as a sustainable, accessible protein source and having it documented in government policy.

I have been extraordinarily fortunate to attend the Commission for the Status of Women (CSW) at the United Nations in New York. Here, I have spoken on many issues facing RRR women in Australia with a focus on the rights of women to own, grow and access food and potable water in their own right. Growing up in awe of the work the UN does, and then speaking in those hallowed rooms, is probably the scariest thing I have ever done. Yet I'm so glad I did, as it opened a whole new world and direction for me. It has taken me to New York and Bangkok, working with both

by Leonie Noble

the Australian government on gender equality and equity and on human rights. Sometimes this was on official government delegations and sometimes with civil society on Australian delegations to fight for the rights of women.

As Hillary Clinton once famously said, "Human rights are women's rights and women's rights are human rights." And whilst I'm not a bra burning feminist, the work I do on and with the civil society Australian international language team in this space makes a difference in a global context. Australia plays an important role in crafting international documents and gaining the agreement of signatories to international statements so countries may be held accountable in the international court. The documents and statements that Australia is a signatory to form part of an important advocacy platform for all of us. So, although human rights can be at times soul destroying and a constant fight, it is also interesting and stimulating work.

Over the years, it has been a constant struggle to juggle being in positions that have access to change-makers and opportunities on a global scale with those on a smaller scale in my own community and are so close to my heart.

You really can't do it all. I know I can give 100% personally but instead of trying to be everything to everybody, I have been specific in understanding what I believe needs to change at both the macro and micro levels. Then I look at the opportunities offered in each so I can judge whether they will have the positive impact that is needed.

From the early days, I have always believed you need to have more than an idea or a project or an education to make a difference, no matter how big or small. In the case of making gender equality a reality, you also need to have an unshakable belief in what needs to

by Leonie Noble

happen. You need this unshakable belief so you can say "I am a believer."

I believe that if you can give someone a voice or create a place at the table, you should.

I believe that if you have the determination and passion to effect change, you should.

And I agree with Simon Sinek's belief...

> "If a movement is to have an impact, then it has to belong to those who join it, not those who lead it."

I believe we should listen more before we speak, and we need to learn how to deliver a message in many different ways as we all learn and are impacted differently.

And most importantly, we need to be brave. Not everything will be comfortable. Not every position is easy. We all need to be able to give and take feedback in a way that is meaningful. It doesn't matter what level we take on, in any role there are times you need to be able to make hard decisions that won't make you popular and you need to be able to back yourself when you do. As leaders, we need to be able to have those difficult gut-wrenching conversations. They are a necessary part of the gig.

Malcolm Fraser once said, "Life wasn't meant to be easy." I say to you now, neither is leadership. It's a constant juggle of personalities, issues and often, personal insecurities. But it's also a vehicle to make a difference.

So, to finish, I ask you this... what do you believe in? Does it make a difference to the work you do in a meaningful way? Does it inform the decisions you make? Will your beliefs help you to stand up for those who have no voice or who need help to have a better life? Do your beliefs help you sleep at night?

by Leonie Noble

And never, ever be afraid of becoming your version of that argumentative girl from Geraldton who doesn't fit in.

My life, my journey is mine. It will be different for us all and that's what makes humanity so interesting. Everyone has a story. I hope one day I get to hear yours.

Business in Heels' books

Other books in the series

RAW ~ Real Stories from Nine Resilient Women

Shame, Guilt, Ridicule, Poverty, Horror, Impotence, Violence, Fear. Nevertheless, it seems we get an (un)healthy dose of those sometimes too. Mostly, it's not a case of if... it's when. And while you can surround yourself with positive and like-minded people to help you through, when all is said and done, it's those lonely hours between 2am and 4am when we often find ourselves facing our demons.

RAW explores the trials of nine everyday women who chose to carry on. Sure, there's some baggage... but that's a hell of a lot healthier than being continuously beaten up by those demons.

Feeling like it's all about you? It's not. Take comfort from the stories of others who've walked a few miles on some windy, rocky roads through their own barren wastelands... and emerged stronger, sharper and ready to get on with it.

Need a new perspective? RAW may help set you on a happier path.

Get your copy now

businessinheels.net/raw-book

Business in Heels' books

Rise Above ~ beyond ordinary

These are eight remarkable women

Each has a story to tell

Each has a message of hope to share

This collection of stories show the might and power of eight women who refuse to be beaten. Together, they have endured hardship, broken marriages, health crises, catastrophes, self-doubt, parental discouragement, business failure and more.

Yet with grit and determination and fire in their bellies, they have forged on and rebuit their lives, businesses and careers. Their courage, resilience and deep sense of purpose has enabled each to find her path.

Get your copy now

businessinheels.net/riseabove-book-order

Business in Heels' books

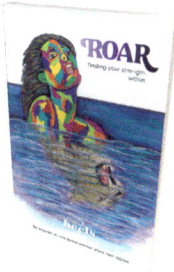

Roar ~ finding your strength, within.

These nine courageous women have gone out of their way to tell it like it is. Prepare to be shocked, to cry, to admire their bravery. Prepare to shake your head in disbelief. Whatever your reaction, know that these women are no longer prepared to cork it, sit still and look pretty.
Prepare to hear them... *Roar!*

Get your copy now

businessinheels.net/roarbook

Inspire

Business in Heels' books

Renewal ~ Real stories, real advice from eleven remarkable women

Life throws curve balls at us all.

Some we see coming so we duck and weave in time to avoid them. Others hit us smack in the face and leave a lasting scar. Others we see collide with loved ones and we're paralysed by the ricochet.

There is no single path life's lessons take to us, no orbit you can sail to avoid them and no chance they will ever arrive at a good time. The only guarantee is that life will send the experiences and it's up to us to learn from them. Moreover, the generous among us will share their lessons so others may avoid their pain.

This is the story of... *Renewal*

Get your copy now

businessinheels.net/renewal-book

Inspire

www.ingramcontent.com/pod-product-compliance
Lightning Source LLC
Chambersburg PA
CBHW042047290426
44109CB00006B/141